A Load of Old Balls

by Simon Inglis

To Martyn & Amanda
Have a ball !
Simon

ENGLISH HERITAGE

A Load of Old Balls © English Heritage 2005

English Heritage is the government's statutory advisor on all aspects of the historic environment

23 Savile Row, London W1X 1AB
www.english-heritage.org.uk

Design by Doug Cheeseman and Jörn Kröger
Production by Jackie Spreckley at Malavan Media, creators of the Played in Britain series
www.playedinbritain.co.uk

Printed by Zrinski, Croatia
ISBN: 0 9547445 27
Product Code: 51131

Above Spot the ball – seen without their leather covers these old hockey ball 'quilts' consist of a baked kernel of cork, wrapped tightly in layers of worsted, cork and latex. For the inside view, see page 13.

Previous page Another batch of cricket balls leaves the Kent factory of Duke & Son in 1931.

Contents

A load of old balls

There are loads of old balls in Britain. Gathering mould in the back of cupboards, stuck up in trees or in the rafters of cathedrals, forgotten in lofts or garages. Buried amid the detritus of history, they turn up in all sorts of places.

We all have at least one old ball knocking around somewhere in our house or garden.

In fact the oldest known balls in Britain, and perhaps even the world, are a set of three beautifully crafted wood, leather and papyrus balls, from ancient Egypt, c.2000 BC, held by the British Museum. But these are imported artefacts. They were never booted or bounced, bowled or biffed on these shores.

On these pages we concentrate instead on balls that we know for sure were, in the spirit of this series, either Made in Britain, or at the very least Played in Britain.

Balls are so easily disregarded. Or rather, we follow their movements so closely during the course of a game that we tend to overlook their qualities and characteristics simply as designed objects, as manufactured articles.

Balls are so immediately identifiable – their purpose so transparently obvious – that they are, paradoxically, almost invisible.

We even describe them as 'dead' when they cross the touchline or if play is brought to a halt.

It is therefore time to bring back to life the finest of our old balls, to dust them down and peer into their depths. To feel their mass and their weight and, above all, to remind ourselves of what they were for, how they were made, and what their stories can tell us about our nation's wonderfully rich and diverse sporting heritage.

Of course balls are in no way a peculiarly British phenomenon. The ancient Greeks toyed with them at least seven thousand years ago, while balls played an important role in the religious, social and militaristic rites of several early civilisations. The Chinese, for example, are known to have played a form of indoor football

In order to form a just estimation of the character of any particular people, it is absolutely necessary to investigate the Sports and Pastimes most generally prevalent among them.
The Sports and Pastimes of the People of England
Joseph Strutt, 1801

as early as the 3rd century BC, while the Mayans and Aztecs of central America built extremely sophisticated ball courts for their own unique brand of ball game, with stone circles placed high up on the side walls to serve as goals.

Even many of the sports that we consider to be quintessentially British, such as golf, billiards, tennis and cricket, have their origins firmly rooted in mainland Europe.

The peoples of this island, it must also be conceded, have been relatively slow to cotton onto the use of those technologies upon which the development of balls has so often depended. The use of air pumps to blow up animal bladders, for example, was known to the Romans, the Chinese and to 16th century Italians. And yet as late as the 19th century we come across the wife of Richard Lindon, a ball maker in Rugby, whose death was blamed on her daily exertions from blowing up bladders using the stems of clay pipes and pure lung power.

In a very real sense the history of balls is intimately bound up with the history of materials.

In 1496, when Christopher Columbus returned from the West Indies with the first rubber balls ever seen in Europe, Spanish observers were said to have been astonished and delighted in equal measure. Never before had they seen such bounce. Yet there is evidence of the Mayans using rubber as far back as 1600 BC.

Without rubber, and particularly vulcanised rubber after 1839, there would have been no lawn tennis – because the stuffed balls used in the original form of tennis would not bounce on grass – and no regulation sized footballs.

▲ Cork, worsted, hemp, brown oats, suet, lard, alum, stale ale and dragon's blood – these were just a few of the ingredients listed in 1853 by Tom Twort of Southborough, Kent, for the manufacture of cricket balls. Ball makers of the pre-industrial age were forever experimenting with organic materials. Early tennis balls were stuffed with hair (even human hair), wool and cloth. Billiard balls were made from ivory, while golf would hardly have got off the ground had it not been for goose feathers. This Playfair cricket ball from the early 1890s catalogue of HJ Gray & Sons was made from cork, worsted, leather and cat-gut.

▲ Not all old balls are readily identifiable. A hoard of wooden and leather balls discovered in a well in Lincoln, for example, might have been used in any number of games, while this stuffed curiosity, on display at Twickenham's Rugby Museum, defies categorisation. Around 20cm in diameter, but weighing in at a hefty 1.8kg, it is too heavy for any kicking or handling game. Could it instead have been used for a form of mob football? Another obstacle to identification is that leather from before the late 19th century, when chrome was first used in tanning, is very hard to date.

Why is the rugby ball shaped the way it is? Again because before vulcanised rubber the type of pig's bladder most commonly used dictated the ovoid form of the ball.

Another wonder material discovered in the Caribbean was lignum vitae, the hardest, densest wood known to man. First imported in the 16th century it soon replaced ash, yew and other native woods traditionally used for making bowls, which was then virtually the national sport in England (as evinced by the apocryphal story of Sir Francis Drake playing on even as the Spanish Armada approached in 1588).

Sport and industry, meanwhile, have long enjoyed a symbiotic relationship.

As we shall later learn, it was concern for the supply of ivory tusks for billiard balls that indirectly led to the development of celluloid in the 1870s, which in turn provided the developers of table tennis with just the ball they had been searching for in the 1890s. Indeed this gradual transition from organic materials to composites – a process that brought us wonderfully branded American products such as Bonzoline, Evertrue and Mineralite (with its 'mysterious rubber compound') – is a major thread running throughout our story, and continues until the present day. (Many a modern football and rugby ball contains, as a result, no leather at all.)

At the same time, as urban workers and the middle classes found more time and cash for leisure pursuits, developing industries were always on the lookout for new markets to exploit. Thus we find Scottish potteries virtually inventing the game of carpet bowls during the 1840s, and, not long after, German glass manufacturers perfecting the mass production of colourful marbles that no small boy could possibly resist. Vast quantities of these baubles found their way onto Britain's streets, having served conveniently as ballast for ships.

Hardly a sport or pastime was untouched by the fruits of science or industry. Just a few examples will suffice by way of illustration.

Before the availability of manufactured footballs of the appropriate weights and pressures in the late 19th century, the idea of heading a ball would have seemed absurd. Until the introduction of machine lathes in 1871, by the Glasgow manufacturer Thomas Taylor, it was virtually impossible for bowls to be produced with a precisely calculated bias. And in golf, only when mass production of durable, affordable rubber-cored balls began in the early 20th century could the game be truly embraced by anyone outside the monied classes.

Golf is a prime example of a sport whose spread beyond these shores was to have major consequences for British manufacturers.

For 400 years or so all golf balls were made in Scotland, the majority by cottage industries based around St Andrews, Edinburgh and Musselburgh. However once gutta percha replaced feathers as the prime material for ball manufacture in the 1850s, and the game expanded thereafter, these small companies soon found their market share plummeted.

Similarly with cricket balls. For over 100 years a cluster of manufacturers based in and around Tonbridge and Southborough in Kent dominated

Until the spread of cricket, football and rugby bowls was virtually the national sport. But its modern form owes much to Scottish ingenuity.

William Gilbert's family firm in Rugby made rugby balls from 1823 until its sale in 1978. Its former workshop in St Matthew's Street – where this photograph was taken in the 1930s – is now the home of the Webb Ellis Rugby Museum.

the business. But once cricket gained popularity in the colonies it was only a matter of time before rival makers entered the field. When the MCC went on tour to Australia in 1946 and found that local balls were to be used in preference to standard British ones, the writing was well and truly on the wall. From a total of at least 20 ball makers operating in Britain before 1914, today only two survive, Reader and Duke, and both outsource most of their production to India and the Far East.

It is the same tale for makers of footballs, rugby balls and tennis balls.

So it is that the pages of this book are littered with the names of once prominent British ball manufacturers – the Nikes, Pumas, Mitres and Reeboks of their time – who have long since gone out of business.

Here are just a few names to match up against those old balls you might have lying in your attic.

FH Ayres of Aldersgate, London, were one of the leading sports equipment manufacturers of the late 19th century. Established in 1810 and equally renowned for their rocking horses, wooden toys and games, Ayres supplied tennis balls to the All England Club at Wimbledon from 1879-1902.

Harry Gradidge, founded in 1870, also made a range of balls and equipment at their factory in Woolwich, not far from that of Jefferies & Malings, specialists in tennis, rackets and fives, and participants in the 1851 Great Exhibition, as were Lillywhite & Sons of Islington and the Rugby leathergoods firm of William Gilbert, who of course made rugby balls.

Henry Malings later set up on his own account, as did another former Jefferies & Malings worker, TH Prosser, who opened a works making rackets and balls in Pentonville Road in 1866.

Also established during this period was William Sykes. Originally a saddler, Sykes started making footballs in 1870, before developing what has been described as possibly the largest sports equipment factory in the world, the Yorkshire Athletic Manufactory, in Horbury, near Leeds.

John Wisden, a name more associated nowadays with his annual cricketers' almanack, was a manufacturer too, with a shop in Cranbourn Street, near Leicester Square, and a factory in Mortlake, close to that of Taylor-Rolph, who were makers of bowls.

Other major retailers of sports equipment whose branded balls were once to be found in Christmas stockings and club pavilions around the nation included Paisley's in Glasgow, Frank Suggs in Liverpool, William Shillcock in Birmingham, and in London, Gamages, famous for their footballs and model trains.

But while all these names are now confined to history books and the catalogues of auction houses, there are notable survivors from within the British ball making industry.

Thomas Taylor are still in business in Glasgow, making composite bowls (now in brightly coloured melamine), while in Liverpool the Clare Group produces bowls branded as Drake's Pride. Established in 1912, Clare are also well known as makers of billiards and snooker equipment, having acquired or incorporated over the years many of the best known firms in that sphere,

Displaying their wares at a 1938 trade fair, Jabez Cliff were one of over 80 leather working firms in Walsall. In the 1920s they turned out 20,000 footballs a year, including the 'Globe', which was used in the 1923 Cup Final and at the 1928 Olympics. The family-run company has also made balls for rounders and fives, but is better known today as supplier of saddles to the Queen.

▲ This set of 'Crystalate' billiard balls from 1911 was designed to help players learn which part of the ball to strike for the desired effect. Crystalate was a form of celluloid, developed in America to replace ivory when supplies dwindled. Early trials of the balls during the 1860s suffered one major drawback, however. If struck in a certain way they had a tendency to explode. A saloon proprietor in Colorado complained to the makers that he did not so much mind the loss of the balls as the fact that every time it happened, 'instantly every man in the room pulled a gun'.

such as Thos. Padmore of Birmingham (founded in 1830), Peradon of Andover (1830), and most famously of all, the venerable London company, Thurston & Co., established by the furniture maker John Thurston in 1799 and the creators of the billiard table as we know it today.

Even older than Thurston's is the Edenbridge firm of John Jaques, whose name crops up several times in our story. Founded in London in 1795 and thought to be oldest sports and games manufacturer in the world – and one which, remarkably, remains in family ownership – Jaques has several claims to prominence, not least that it invented, appropriately enough, the card game Happy Families, shaped the look of modern chess sets, and was a leading promoter of both croquet, in the 1860s, and table tennis in the early 1900s.

Also controlled by members of its founding family is the firm of Grays, now of Robertsbridge, but for many years based in Cambridge.

Grays were set up in 1855 by HJ 'Harry' Gray, a printer's son who learnt to make balls at the real tennis court attached to the University Arms Tavern in Cambridge and later became the World Rackets champion. Although better known as makers of rackets and cricket bats, Grays produced a range of balls for tennis and hockey, and over the years absorbed such firms as John Wisden, Taylor Rolph and, for a short period, the oldest cricket ball brand in the world, Duke's of Penshurst (now independently owned and based in east London).

In 2002 Grays also acquired the Gilbert brand of rugby balls, of which more later.

A similar string of acquisitions characterises the history of perhaps the best known British manufacturer of all, Slazenger.

Originally a firm of tailors and umbrella makers, founded in Manchester by Jewish refugees in the early 19th century, Slazenger started producing tennis sets from a factory in Woolwich – clearly a popular spot for sports manufacturers – in the 1880s, and in 1902 took over as official supplier of balls to Wimbledon from their rivals FH Ayres, whom they later bought up in 1940, along with the Yorkshire firm of William Sykes. Nine years earlier they had also taken over their Woolwich neighbours Gradidge.

That left only one major competitor in the general balls business, and that was the rubber giant, Dunlop, with whom Slazenger amalgamated in 1958. However Slazenger retain their independent status as suppliers to Wimbledon – a relationship now over a century old – and, as we will later read, they also made the football with which England won the World Cup in 1966.

Also featured is a ball used in another of England's famous World Cup victories – that of rugby, in 2003. But although it bears the familiar name of Gilbert and is marketed by Grays, along with the majority of balls now sold by British companies, it was actually made overseas.

In that respect, the old balls we are about to parade bear a resonance that carries far beyond the realms of sport. They are historic tokens of great British invention, craftsmanship and, above all, our innate love of fun and games.

We should guard them well.

▲ Cork, cotton, latex and leather – not perhaps as exotic as Thomas Twort's recipe for cricket balls in 1853 (*see page 7*), but in essence the structure of this 1980s hockey ball would be familiar to any ballmaker, whether for hockey or cricket, from the last 200 years. Apart from this form of cored ball, there are five other basic types: stuffed balls and solid wooden balls, the most commonly used before the mid 19th century; solid rubber or synthetic composite balls (such as used in bowls, snooker and increasingly in golf); inflatable balls (football and rugby) and air filled balls (tennis).

Hull half-bowl c.1280-1300

We begin with what is thought to be the oldest purpose-made sporting ball known in Britain. And a curious object it is too. For a start, it is not a sphere, but oblate in shape. Made of solid wood, it also appears to have been turned on a lathe.

When excavated in the 1980s – from the site of a medieval timbered hall on the corner of High Street and Blackfriargate – it was assumed to be a bowling ball, or at least, the remnants of one, for one side is flat, as if a section had split away.

Archaeological evidence from the site confirms that it dates from the late 13th century, which ties in with the earliest recorded bowling greens in Britain; at Southampton and Chesterfield, both dating from the 1290s. However, further analysis suggests that the Hull bowl was crafted in this odd shape deliberately, not for a green but for a form of skittles played indoors in confined spaces.

'Half-bowl' was one of several games prohibited by Edward IV in 1477, presumably because it distracted men from archery practice and fostered gambling. (The other banned games were closh and kyles, of which more on the next page.)

Writing in 1801, Joseph Strutt described half-bowl as a game in which 12 pins were set up in a circle, with one other in the centre and two outside. When released by a practised player, owing to its eccentric bias the half-bowl travelled in a wide, curving arc. The aim was to knock down all the pins, but only after the half-bowl had cleared the pin at the far side of the circle.

According to Strutt the game was known in Hertfordshire as rolly-polly. Indeed similar versions are still played today, as *rolle bolle* in Belgium, *pierbol* in Holland and *media bola* in Spain. Given that the grounds of the hall from which the half-bowl was dug up had monastic connections, it is therefore likely that the game had arrived on Britain's east coast from Europe.

If so, it is only one of many imported games we shall encounter. Half-bowl, half-British. But wholly enigmatic all the same.

Diameter 10cm
Weight 400g

Ironmacannie kyles c.16th-17th century

They were discovered in 1835 in a peat moss, just outside the Galloway village of Ironmacannie; three rough-hewn kyles and a ball, possibly made from pine, though clearly not by a craftsman. Possibly medieval. Certainly no later than 1650.

The word kyle itself comes from the French *quille*, for skittle. But in what type of game might these homespun relics have been used?

So diverse is the variety of skittles known in Europe throughout the ages that we can only guess. In Germany, as early as the 3rd and 4th centuries, a *kegel* was a flat-bottomed club used partly in self defence, partly by monks who told peasants that each *kegel* represented a sin that they had to topple with a stone. In later incarnations – in England variously referred to as kayles, keiles and later, Aunt Sally – instead of a stone or ball, a stick or truncheon was thrown.

Some games, such as closh and Dutch pins, used between six to nine skittles, one of them a 'kingpin'. Sometimes the ball was thrown, or lobbed from between the legs. In other versions, such as half-bowl, the ball was cheese-shaped. In loggats, bones took the place of skittles.

But what links all these variations across the centuries was their association with drinking and gambling, that age-old combination of 'beer and skittles'. Unsurprisingly therefore, such games were frequently listed amongst those activities outlawed by King and Kirk alike, whether it was to concentrate minds on archery practice or holy worship, or simply to discourage mob gatherings.

In Scotland such puritanical strictures reached a peak in the decades before the Restoration in 1660. Typical of these was a fine of 10 shillings on anyone in Perthshire caught playing at kyles on the Sabbath. Indeed it may well have been a similar injunction which persuaded the owners of these homespun kyles to hide them away until the coast was clear. Perhaps they hid them too well. Or did they make themselves a better set? In any event, their loss is indubitably our gain.

Common bowling-alleys are privy mothers that eat up the credit of many idle citizens, whose gaynes at home are not able to weigh down their losses abroad: whose shoppes are so farre from maintaining their play that their wives and children cry out for bread, and go to bedde supperlesse oft in the yeere.
The School of Abuse, Stephen Gossen, 1579

Diameter 17.8cm
Weight 1320g

Real tennis ball 16th century

You have heard of 'hair of the dog'. Well that is exactly what was used to stuff this Tudor leather tennis ball, discovered in the rafters of Westminster Hall in 1922. Other fillings from the period include moss (as in a 15th century ball found at Baynards Castle, Blackfriars), shredded leather (found in a well in Lincoln) and, according to Shakespeare's *Much Ado About Nothing*, human hair (or beard clippings, to be exact).

So perturbed was Louis XI of France by the use of sub-standard fillings that in 1480 he issued a list of banned substances; among them sand, ground chalk, lime and metal shavings. Only wool wadding and good hide were to be sanctioned.

This was important stuff, quite literally. Before the advent of air-filled rubber balls allowed tennis to move outdoors onto turf in the 1860s, the game depended on the interaction of a dry ball on a stone floor. The workmanship of the *paumiers* – the court professionals who were also tasked with making balls – was therefore paramount.

Consequently, until the 1590s French balls were preferred by English players (much to the ire of 'Artificers, Handcrafty men and women' who had, a century earlier, protested that they were being 'gretely empoveryshed' by foreign imports).

Tennis itself changed significantly in the 16th century. Instead of striking the ball by hand, rackets now became commonplace. Thus emerged a new and tougher ball, using a core made from tightly wound cloth, which was then wrapped in tape (a method first noted in 1581 and in essence still used today). Cloth covers, easily renewable, also replaced leather covers by around 1600.

With that in mind, and because we have no record of tennis being played at Westminster after c.1520, we can estimate that this particular ball dates from the early 16th century, if not before.

Thanks to the efforts of a modern *paumier* at Hampton Court we can also see (*left*) what the ball would have looked like when new. Only this time, we are assured, the dog was spared.

Diameter c.4cm
Weight c.45g

Stirling Castle ball c.16th century

When workmen found this small leather ball hidden within the Queen's Chamber at Stirling Castle in the 1970s, little interest was stirred. With its dried up bladder still inside the casing, the ball was merely classified under 'leather goods' and deposited in the local museum.

More recent research by the Scottish Football Museum, however, suggests that it may be of considerable historic significance.

The ball's age may partly be deduced from the location of its concealment, behind a wall erected as part of James V's reconstruction of the castle between 1537-42. From the Accounts of the Lord High Treasurer during the reign of James IV, dated 11 April 1497, we also find an order from Stirling, 'giffin to Jame Dog to by fut ballis to the King.'

So might this ball be one of Mr Dog's?

Football was certainly being played at this time in Scotland, at least by the brave (as depicted below). Sir David Lindsay, a satirist in the court of James V, listed 'futeball' among the pursuits of his protagonist Squyer Meldrum, while during Mary Queen of Scots' imprisonment at Carlisle in 1568, according to a letter from Francis Knollys, '20 of her retinue played at football before her for two hours very strongly, nimbly, and skilfully...'

'Theyr fairer play,' wrote Knollys, was owing to 'the smalness of theyr balle'.

But it is the very smallness of the Stirling ball which has led the National Museum of Scotland to suggest that it was not used for football, but for *pallone*, a tennis-like game in which players strike the ball with wooden sheaths attached to their forearms. Popular at European courts in the 16th century and still played in Italy today, *pallone* – the Italian for ball or balloon – uses a bladder-inflated ball similar in size to the Stirling example.

If this is a *pallone* it adds intriguing evidence to what is already known of Scotland's close ties with European fashion during the Stewart period.

But if it is indeed a football, it is, as far as we know, the oldest surviving example in the world.

Brissil brawnis and broken banis
Strife, discord and waistit wanis
Crookit in eild, syne halt withal –
These are the bewties of the fute-ball
16th century Scottish rhyme

Diameter varies from 14-16cm
Weight 125g

Caich balls c.1690–1830

Another Scottish find, this time in July 1954 from the tower of St Salvator's College, St Andrews, as follows: a single leather ball, roughly 6.8cm in diameter, apparently stuffed with wool, part of the stitching being loose; three slightly larger balls of similar construction, but in varying stages of disintegration; three smaller balls, made from wound woollen yarn; three corks, one wrapped in fabric, one possibly a fishing float, together with sundry scraps of wool and fabric.

Response: for 45 years the finds gathered dust in the stores of the University of St Andrews, until in 1999 they were rediscovered and sent for analysis to a textile research laboratory in York.

Materials identified: sheep's wool, goat's hair and flax, all Scottish in origin, coloured by traditional natural dyes of purple, blue, navy, brown, ochre, green and yellow.

Date: taking into account both the materials and the history of the buildings at St Salvator's, from between 1690 and 1830.

Purpose: a game popular with students during this period was caich, later known as handball or fives, thought to have arrived from the Netherlands in the 15th century. Two or more players would strike the ball with their hands against any large wall that also had clear, flat ground in front (and hopefully few or no windows). Such a ballcourt was known as a cachpule, cachpoole or kaithspell.

Construction: this being St Andrews, the cradle of golf, there were plenty of local ball makers, using leather casings packed tightly under pressure with boiled feathers, rags, or, as here, wool or hair stuffed around a cork core. In their prime, these balls would have offered excellent bounce, a key requirement for caich.

Location: gambling was a key element of caich. It is therefore possible that the balls were hidden in the tower after a clampdown by college seniors.

Conclusion: all museum stores to be checked forthwith, lest there be other old balls out there, forgotten in the shadows.

Typical diameter 6.8-7cm

Barnes Bowling Club, London

Lignum Vitae woods c.19th century

No one at the Barnes Bowling Club knows how old the assorted bowls, or 'woods' stacked away in their pavilion actually are. That is one of the wonders of lignum vitae, the hardwood from which bowls have been made since the timber was discovered on the island of San Domingo in around 1500. Certainly they are a century old, maybe more, as is the ivory jack also seen here. The Barnes club itself formed in 1725.

Lignum vitae, the 'wood of life' – it was once thought, wrongly, to cure syphilis – is the densest wood known to man. Because of its high fat and resin content it is also self-lubricating and virtually impervious to water, making it ideal for ship's propellors, Mosquito aircraft, chisel handles, gavels… and of course bowls (which are made from the dark centre of the trunk, shown below).

Since the invention of synthetic, or composite bowls in 1931, and, more recently, the banning of lignum vitae imports, only one in ten British bowlers still uses traditional woods, rather as some music lovers stay loyal to vinyl.

A vital characteristic of bowls is their 'bias'. This, determined by their slightly oblate shape – though for a time also by the insertion of lead weights – makes them roll in a curved trajectory.

In flat green bowls, for example, a typical bias is labelled 3. But the Barnes woods have a bias of 12 or 13, which means they curve in almost a complete semi-circle (shades of that Hull half-bowl). Allied to this quirk, the club's green, tucked behind the Sun Inn, rises up at its edges, with games played diagonally, from corner to corner.

After the rules of flat green bowls were first codified by a Glasgow solicitor in 1848, such local eccentricities were virtually ironed out of the game. But not at Chesterfield, where the green is said to date back to the 13th century, nor Lewes, where the game has been played since at least 1658, and certainly not at Barnes.

In some maverick quarters, it is not only the woods that remain impervious to change.

Diameter 11-12.5cm
Weight 1360g

William Ward's cricket ball 1820

William Ward, director of the Bank of England and an MCC regular, was celebrating his 33rd birthday on the day he stepped up at Lord's to face the underarm bowlers of Norfolk – overarm was yet to come – on 24 July 1820. Three bruising days later he was finally dismissed, having swatted the ball around the ground for a record 278 runs.

Small wonder it looks so battered. And yet apart from the fading of its original red dye, Ward's ball looks remarkably similar to those of today.

At its core is the 'quilt', a hard-baked kernel of cork and worsted. Around this are successive layers of thin cork and thread that the ballmaker would have patiently hammered and pressed until the requisite size and weight was attained. Two outer 'cups' of tanned hide then enclosed each half of the quilt. Squeezed together in a vice, these were hand-sewn together by the 'closer' to create the all-important triple seams that have remained a vital tool in the bowler's trade ever since.

But who first arrived at this classic design?

Was it Duke & Son, still the best known name in the business today (albeit no longer in family hands), established in Penshurst, Kent, in 1760, 16 years after cricket's first laws were drafted? Or was it John Small of Petersfield, the cricketing son of a saddler, who made similar balls for both the Hambledon club and the MCC? (Ward's ball, it is thought, may well be one of Small's.)

Whatever, the design was soon adopted by dozens of other manufacturers, the majority in Kent. Eight were in Tonbridge alone (including Wisden and Surridge) and seven in Southborough.

And so for nearly 200 years Kent's ball makers supplied the world, until now, Duke, based in Walthamstow, are the only company left manufacturing balls in Britain. As for Ward, he loved Lord's so dearly that five years after his epic innings he paid £5,000 to save it from developers. How apt then, that his 1820 ball should now rest in the ground's museum, where it is deemed by experts to be the oldest cricket ball in the world.

Diameter 7.16cm
Weight 158g

Royal and Ancient Golf Club of St Andrews

Feathery golf ball c.1850

As the name suggests, a feathery golf ball was one filled with goose or chicken feathers. These had been boiled beforehand and then, with an awl, stuffed tightly into a case made from three stitched pieces of bullhide (the leather itself having already been softened in alum and water). It took no less than one top hat full of feathers to fill each ball.

Once sewn up, the casing was liberally coated in white lead paint, to create a surprisingly tough, elastic ball that travelled considerable distances.

In golf's earliest years, by which we mean the 15th century (when the game spread from the Netherlands to Scotland), the balls were thought to have been made from boxwood, although no examples survive. But from c.1450 onwards the feathery dominated. Many were imported from Holland until, in 1618, James I granted a Scottish maker, James Melvill, a monopoly on their manufacture in return for a cut of the proceeds.

By 1838 it was reckoned that ballmakers in and around St Andrews, the epicentre of the

game, were making 10,000 featheries a year. But it was arduous work. In the workshop of the leading maker, Allan Robertson, a skilled hand might complete only three or four balls per day.

One such man was Tom Morris (1821-1908), later to become Scotland's most revered golfer. (His shop is still in business, facing the 18th hole of the St Andrews course.) As can be seen, Morris stamped on each ball both his name and its weight, 28 penny weights. This was a unit of the Troy system, used otherwise for weighing gold.

In fact, surviving featheries can be worth far more than their weight in gold. One, made around 1840 by David Marshall of Leith, fetched just short of £20,000 at auction in 1995.

Its original cost would have been nearer 3-4 shillings. But even this was prohibitively costly for the time, and it was only when featheries were superceded by more affordable, mass produced *gutta percha* balls from the 1850s onwards, that golf could emerge as the popular sport it is today.

The feathers harden and the leather swells;
He crams and sweats, yet crams and urges more,
Till scarce the turgid globe contains its store.
The Goff, by Thomas Mathison, 1743

Diameter 4.5cm
Weight 43.6g

Gilbert's rugby ball 1851

Of 13,000 exhibitors represented at the 1851 Great Exhibition in Hyde Park, 25 manufactured sports equipment. Of these, ten related to angling, nine to cricket and five to archery. This splendid canopy, on stand no. 187, was crafted by William Gilbert of Rugby. Originally boot and shoemakers, Gilberts had supplied balls to Rugby School since at least the 1820s, and by 1851 were based in St Matthew's Street, where the present day museum is located. Leather panels on the canopy's uprights display the crests of all the school houses.

Rugby was a little known game at this stage, having developed, as school lore has it, after a 15 year old pupil, William Webb Ellis, showed a 'fine disregard for the rules' in 1823 by running with the ball in his hands, rather than, as custom dictated, retiring back then punting it forward. The veracity of this tale has been much disputed since, though there is evidence, not least from *Tom Brown's Schooldays*, that the handling game did become accepted practice during the 1830s.

Cambridge University adopted rugby in 1839, but otherwise, in 1851 this oddly-shaped ball would have been regarded by the general public more with curiosity than general recognition. Certainly the ball handled by Webb Ellis would have been round, or at least nearly round.

So why the distinct oval by 1851? The likeliest theory is that it was dictated by the shape of the pigs' bladders favoured by Gilbert, which resulted in a ball better suited to drop and place kicking *over*, rather then *under* the crossbar. Following the introduction of rubber bladders in 1862 – by Gilbert's rival, Richard Lindon (whose wife, as we read earlier, suffered greatly from blowing up bladders using lung power alone) – it then became more uniformly oval and thus easier to handle.

And so the Gilbert family business continued until it was finally bought up in 1978. The brand is now owned by Grays of Cambridge, who formed in 1855 and whose latest Gilbert ball is also part of a great exhibition, as will later be revealed…

Length 29cm
Diameter at centre 21.6cm
Weight 408g

Carpet bowls 1850s

Ceramics, one might assume, have no place amid the rough and tumble of sport and games.

But that did not deter William Gaunt Jnr of Glasgow, Manufacturer of China Figures and Ornaments, Toys, Marbles &c..

'Parlour Bowling', he announced in an advert of 1846, 'is the *sine qua non* in fashionable circles'. This 'truly delightful and exhilirating game' possessed 'all the enjoyments of curling, without causing over excitement.' It was, moreover, 'an amusement in which the ladies can participate'.

A simple adaptation of lawn bowls, carpet bowls offered Scottish potteries an ideal entrée into the burgeoning market for domestic leisure. All players needed, at 3s a set, was 12 bowls, a jack and a strip of carpet, felt or matting.

Had a joiner hatched the idea no doubt the bowls would have been made of wood. Instead, not only were they ceramic but, in order to appeal to feminine sensibilities, they were finished in a variety of ornate patterns and colourful glazes – in

stripes, plaids, sponge prints and agateware – so that even if one never actually played, the bowls were in themselves objects of curiosity and allure.

These carpet bowls and the white jack, from the late 19th century, were probably made in one of numerous Scottish potteries active from the 1850s onwards, the leading exponents being the Fife Pottery and Links Pottery, both in Kirkaldy. Other examples have been traced to potteries in Portobello, Glasgow, Sunderland and Staffordshire.

Although more robust than they appear, the game's rules required the bowls to be pushed with a cupped hand, rather than bowled or thrown.

Alas for the potteries, the arrival of synthetic bowls from Australia in the 1930s put an end to the trade. But not to the popularity of the bowls themselves. A thriving antiques market, together with prized museum collections in both York and Fife, have happily guaranteed their survival as perhaps the most lustrous of all old balls ever to have been made, and played, in Britain.

Typical diameter 7.6 - 9.1cm
Typical weight 480 - 790g

Cassiobury croquet set 1869–70

Best known in fashionable circles for his lavish house parties and energetic private life – he was 78 when he married a third time – the sixth Earl of Essex, Arthur Algernon Capel (1803-92), was an ardent convert to croquet on its introduction to Britain, from Ireland, in the 1850s.

Although croquet's various antecedents are believed to have gone back centuries, a major factor in its emergence at this time was the invention of the lawn mower; a device which allowed even humble homeowners to emulate the smooth swards of the country house set.

And who better to promote the new lawn game than one of London's leading socialites? Thus in 1863, the Earl of Essex started manufacturing croquet sets at sawmills on his Cassiobury Park estate in Hertfordshire (now part of Watford). He also issued a rulebook, only to be sued for plagiarism by another croquet convert, the Irish author and adventurer, Captain Mayne Reid, in a highly publicised court case in 1864. (A further

rulebook, issued also in 1864 by the manufacturer John Jaques, went on to sell 100,000 copies.)

This Cassiobury set, dating from 1869-70, comprises eight mallets, seven milled boxwood balls (one is missing), ten single hoops, and a double hoop, or 'cage', in the centre of which a bell would tinkle as the ball passed through (a frippery rarely found in other sets). Croquet hoops then were twice the width of the balls.

Ultimately, croquet's golden era was short-lived. Lawn tennis, deemed a more exciting game, particularly for chaps, had all but colonised the nation's croquet lawns by 1880. Cassiobury House, meanwhile, was sold to pay off the family's debts in 1920. But in 1937 croquet returned to its former grounds, by then converted into a public park, where it continues today.

And should anyone doubt the game still, consider this. A modern croquet hoop is now just 3mm wider than the ball. Not much scope for error, therefore, and certainly not for partying.

Diameter 9.2cm
Weight 382g

Rubber ball 1874

If croquet owes its emergence to the lawn mower, lawn tennis must be forever indebted to Charles Goodyear, an impoverished American inventor whose experiments with rubber, initially conducted whilst in gaol for debt, led to his discovery, in 1839, of the process he called vulcanisation. Until then natural rubber had turned sticky in hot temperatures and brittle in cold. Now it could retain its spring, whatever the season.

Goodyear's name has since lived on mainly in relation to tyres. But in sport, vulcanisation had a profound effect, not least in billiards, where it ended the need for table cushions to be warmed with hot water pans before play could commence.

The old established game of tennis, meanwhile, played indoors by mainly wealthy individuals, had for centuries depended on the slight bounce achieved by stuffed balls on a hard surface. Now, thanks to vulcanisation, from the 1850s onwards German factories started making air-filled rubber balls that offered real bounce, even on grass.

According to most accepted sources the first players to test out these new balls were a solicitor, Harry Gem, and a Spanish trader, Jean Pereira, on Pereira's croquet lawn in Birmingham in 1859.

Apparently one drawback on firmer ground was excessive bounce, requiring some early exponents to pierce the rubber with hot needles.

But it was a leading player of 'real tennis' (as the old game soon became known) who, ironically, did most to influence the eventual form of the ball. Within months of the first set of lawn tennis rules being patented by a Major Walter Clopton Wingfield in 1874, JM Heathcote informed readers of *The Field* that if covered in white flannel – such as was made in Melton Mowbray – the rubber balls bounced more evenly, were more controllable in flight, and easier to see.

And so it was that a combination of American ingenuity, German manufacturing and fine Leicestershire cloth finally put tennis out to grass, where it has prospered ever since.

Diameter 5.6cm
Weight 60g

Old Trafford Bowling Club, Manchester

Blackball 1877

And the next ball on the agenda, gentlemen, is the most dreaded ball of all in sporting circles.

Its use is time honoured. In ancient Athens citizens could banish an individual by voting with a potsherd, or *ostrakon* – hence 'ostracise' – while the word 'ballot' derives from the Italian *ballotta*, referring to the small balls used in secret votes.

Groucho Marx famously said that he did not want to belong to any club that would accept him as a member. We can only guess at the criteria set by the founding members of the Old Trafford Bowling Club in Manchester.

Their number included corn merchants, timber merchants, a cotton waste dealer, an insurance surveyor, an inn keeper, a cigar merchant, a yeast importer, a printer, engineer, tailor, teacher, tallow chandler, grocer, plumber and painter, stationer, jeweller, someone describing himself as his 'own man', and the manager of the Manchester Cricket Club, based at the Old Trafford cricket ground across the road.

This was a petit-bourgeois club with muscle. Shares cost £5 each. The newly completed mock-Tudor pavilion was one of the finest and most substantial in the industrial north.

Here is how the system originally worked. As the name of each club applicant was read out, members would file past the ballot box, insert their hand into the round opening and, unseen by all, discreetly desposit either a white or a black ball. No matter how many white balls were subsequently counted, one black ball was sufficient for the candidate to be rejected.

In fact the design of the Old Trafford box, and others that survive from the period, suggests that the colour of the ball had ceased to be relevant by this time. Instead, balls were simply dropped into a compartment on either the left or right. A Victorian box at the British Golf Museum has similar drawers marked Admit and Reject.

But the end result was the same. You were either in or out. Accepted, or blackballed.

Harrow School ball c.1870s

Of all the 'muddied oafs' immortalised by Kipling, none were muddier than the boys of Harrow School. The cause was clay; the claggy earth upon which the playing fields were laid when organised sport took hold in the early 19th century.

While other public schools developed their own peculiar strands of football – the handling game at Rugby, the Wall Game at Eton – at Harrow it was the prevalence during winter of thick, unrelenting mud, sometimes reportedly up to a foot deep, that gave rise to a quirky blend of dribbling, catching and kicking.

Such conditions called also for a special type of ball, heavy and tough enough to withstand the mire. Shaped more like a cheese – although the relic shown here would have been nearly spherical when its bladder was inflated – the Harrow ball was closer in form to those cork-stuffed balls used in much longer established folk football games, such as at Atherstone, Ashbourne and Kirkwall (*see page 87*).

In 1887 Montague Shearman described it as 'nothing more than a bladder enclosed in three pieces of thick shoemaker's leather, two being circular and a third a broad strip equal in length to the circumference.' Not a ball for the meek, then, and certainly not for heading.

As it transpired, although no teams outside the school ever played Harrovian 'footer', several of its rules formed the basis of what became known as Association football, or 'soccer', when eventually, in 1863, representatives from various public schools and clubs formed the Football Association in London. An Old Harrovian, Charles Alcock, was the first Secretary of the FA and, in 1872, captain of the first winners of the FA Cup (a competition based on Harrow's Cock House championship).

Since then the school has embraced both soccer and rugger, which are at least played by other schools. But inter-house 'footer' clings on still, albeit a rather different affair since the advent of modern drainage techniques.

When suns are hot and fields are full of shouts and cries that scare you,
You lie in corners dark and dull, an empty lump of air you!
You sit and sulk, a frozen bulk, with pads and bats above you,
Till winter comes again and then, you ugly dear, I love you!
Plump a Lump, by Edward Bowen, 1890

Diameter 27.5cm (at widest)
Weight 820g

Association football 1880s

Given its rather crucial role in the game, and the number of debates that took place concerning the laws of the game in general, it seems odd that no standards were laid down as to the size and weight of footballs until 1872, nine years after the formation of the Football Association.

Finally, at the behest of the Harrow Chequers club, agreement was reached for a size of not less than 27 inches and not more than 28 inches in circumference for balls used in FA Cup ties. Even then the rule was not enforced for other games until 1883, and there was no mention of weight until six years later, when balls for internationals were set at 12-15 ounces. Only in 1905 was the use of leather stipulated, after sundry, but failed attempts to create an all-rubber ball.

The first mass produced ball that met the standards for this period – which saw the formation of the Football League in 1888 and the rapid expansion of the professional game – was the 7 or 8 panel 'button end' ball. Note how discreet the lacing had become, compared, for example with the Harrow ball (see page 41), following complaints about injuries to players.

Button end balls, costing around 10s each, were made by a number of manufacturers, including John Wisden, Lillywhites and William Sykes. But the company we know most about was that of William Shillcock of Birmingham (from whose shop the FA Cup was famously stolen in 1895). By 1905 Shillcock alone was selling 40-50,000 balls a year, around the globe.

'The great point is to get your leather stretched properly,' wrote Shillcock in 1905, although he refused to reveal his methods. He also recommended cowhide as the best material.

To replace the button end ball, in the 1890s Shillcock brought out the 10 panel 'McGregor ball', named after William McGregor, the Scottish founder of the Football League whose draper's shop was round the corner from Shillcock's.

The age of football sponsorship had arrived.

Diameter 22.6cm
Weight 425g

Ivory billiard ball 1890s

Football was not the only sport enjoyed by Mary Queen of Scots (*see page 20*). She also liked a game of billiards, complaining bitterly when the table was removed before her execution in 1587. Mary's balls would have been wooden. But in the following century, a new material emerged.

Unlike wood, ivory balls did not bruise. They were denser and also made a satisfying click when struck. And though rarely completely spherical, and prone to expand in the heat, they were the best a man could get for nigh on 200 years.

Ivory from female elephants was apparently the most suitable, each tusk yielding four to five balls. In 1911 *Billiard Monthly* reported that the London firm, Burroughes & Watts, required 1,140 elephants annually to meet orders. And they supplied perhaps a sixth of the total market.

Fearing that supplies would run out, as early as 1869 a New York manufacturer offered $10,000 to anyone finding an alternative. Duly inspired, an inventor in nearby Albany came up trumps. Experimenting with various formulae for celluloid, John Wesley Hyatt's first synthetic attempts, as we read earlier, tended to explode when clattered together. But eventually he perfected the mix, marketing the new balls under the tradename 'Bonzoline' in USA and 'Crystalate' in Britain.

Seen here is an ivory set made for the game of Pyramid, a precursor of snooker, made by the London firm, Thurstons, in the 1890s. That spot in the centre, by the way, is not painted. It is the nerve that ran through the centre of the tusk.

Billiards from Spain at first deriv'd its name
Both an ingenious and cleanly game
One Gamester leads (the Table green as grass)
And each like Warriors try to gain the Pass
But in the contest e're the Pass be won
Hazards are many into which they run
The Complete Gamester, Charles Cotton, 1674

Diameter 5.25cm
Weight 144g

Table Tennis 1891-1902

When Major Wingfield took out a patent on his new game of lawn tennis in 1874 he gave it the unlikely Greek title of Sphairistikè. But if the name failed to catch on, the game did (*see page 36*), and it was not long before manufacturers sought to emulate its success with an indoor version.

After several failed attempts from both sides of the Atlantic using flat markers, balloons and even 'Tiddledy Winks', in 1890 an English company, David Foster, brought out the first recognisable table tennis set, using strung rackets and a cloth covered rubber ball (*top left*). A year later John Jaques of London launched Gossima. This featured battledores – vellum-covered bats designed for shuttlecocks (*see page 54*) – and a webbed cork ball (*top right*). Both games failed however. Foster's ball had too wild a bounce while Gossima's did not bounce enough.

The breakthrough came in 1900 when, according to one source, a man called James Gibb returned from the USA with some celluloid balls (*bottom left*) that, despite their crude seams, offered a much improved game. Developed, as we read earlier by the American inventor, John Wesley Hyatt, in 1863, celluloid was already in use for billiard balls (as well as for film stock).

Not only were the new balls exceptionally lightweight, when struck by the drum-like surface of a battledore they made a distinct sound, one which led the London store Hamleys to register an inspired brand name for the game in 1900. Soon after they teamed up with John Jaques, who quickly mastered production of what would become the standard ball thereafter (*bottom right*). 'Ping Pong' had arrived.

For a few heady years the world went Ping Pong crazy. At Ping Pong parties people sang Ping Pong ditties, danced the Ping Pong Polka and ate Ping Pong biscuits. This, of course, culminated in Ping Pong diplomacy between the USA and China in 1971; proof that sport and politics can mix if both sides know the name of the game.

Let the timorous turn to their tennis
Or the bowls to which bampkins belong,
But the thing for grown women and men is
The pastime of ping and of pong
The Ballad of Ping Pong, by 'Col. D Streamer', 1905

Diameter 3.8cm (1902 'Ping Pong')
Weight 2g

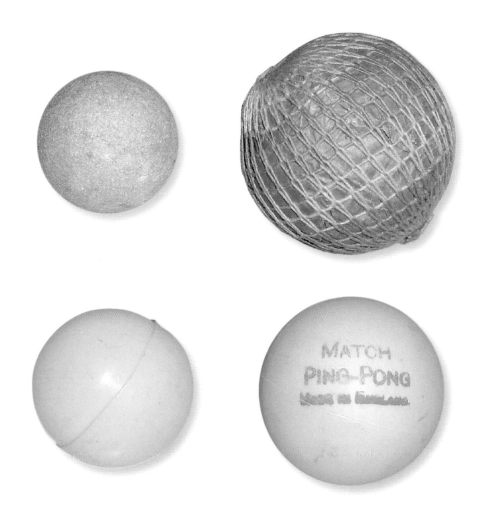

Gutty golf ball 1896

When the venerable ballmaker of St Andrews, Allan Robertson, beheld his first *gutta percha* golf ball in 1848, he was so alarmed at this threat to his profits from featheries (*see page 28*) that he bought up every sample he could find and set fire to them. The sight of his apprentice Tom Morris playing with one filled him with equal fury.

But there could be no turning back.

Originally extracted from a Malaysian gum tree, samples of the sap known as *gutta percha* first arrived in Britain via Singapore in 1843. Soon it was being used to insulate telegraph wires.

Early *gutta percha* golf balls were formed by winding softened strips of the material into a ball which was then heated, pressed into a solid sphere and dropped into cold water to harden. But the new balls did not travel as far as a feathery – on average 170-200 yards compared with 200-220 yards – and had a tendency to split.

Only in the 1870s, after extensive trials, was a more suitable composite of *gutta percha* and vulcanised rubber perfected by the Caledonian Rubber Works in Edinburgh. Known as the 'gutty', this improved type of golf ball would go on to be produced by some 40 companies all over Britain. This one, a Melfort Machine gutty, was made by the WT Henley's Tyre & Rubber Co. of London.

Note its surface pattern. The first *gutta percha* balls were perfectly smooth. However golfers soon noted how the balls' aerodynamics improved once they became nicked. Thus began a series of further trials; first, grooves were hammered by hand, then by machine-cutters. Finally the patterns were formed by mouldings, with each company touting their own designs as the best.

Far more affordable than the feathery, the gutty transformed golf. In 1859, 35 British golf clubs were listed. By 1895 there were 959. By 1901, it has further been estimated, there were 20 million gutty balls in Britain alone. And yet, as we shall discover, like the feathery these too were about to be rendered obsolete...

Diameter 4.3cm
Weight 42.5g

English Bowling Association, Worthing

WG Grace's woods c.1900

Although bowls has been played in Britain since at least the 13th century, its spread in modern times was the direct consequence of two crucial developments, both north of the border.

First came the introduction in the mid 19th century of uniformly level bowling greens, thanks to trials by Scottish greenkeepers of sea-washed turf. Second, in 1871 Thomas Taylor, a long established billiards manufacturer in Glasgow, developed a machine lathe and slate test bed that, for the first time, permitted the production of bowls with a precisely calculated 'bias'.

At last the old game's unpredictability gave way to measured skills, facilitating, as it were, a level playing field on which competition could now thrive. Within a few decades flat green clubs sprang up all over Britain (apart from Lancashire, Yorkshire and the Midlands where 'crown green', played on a cambered turf, remained dominant).

Then in 1900 the flat green fraternity found itself a champion. WG Grace, the greatest cricketer of his age, took up the game at the age of 50, and by 1903 was captain of the England bowls team and president of the English Bowling Association (at whose HQ Grace's woods are now preserved).

Bolstered by this celebrity endorsement, bowls could now slot comfortably alongside lawn tennis into Britain's rapidly expanding suburban matrix. Here was a none too strenuous or time consuming game for both sexes, requiring little equipment (though unlike crown green, flat green players had to wear whites), and free from the taint of gambling that characterised traditional pub bowls.

As for lignum vitae, its days were numbered. In 1914 US bowling alleys started to trial the Mineralite bowl, made from a 'mysterious rubber compound', while for biased bowls the answer turned out to be a phenolformaldehyde composite, invented by Hensel of Australia in 1931. Standard ever since, composites are made today by Drake's Pride in Liverpool and Thomas Taylor in Glasgow, still going strong after 200 years in the trade.

Diameter 12.7–13.9cm
Weight 1463g

Rubber core golf balls 1907-1913

Sometimes technology achieves more than is strictly necessary. Thus Formula 1 cars have to be deliberately slowed down so that existing race tracks can cope. Tennis balls have to be weighted so that serves remain playable. Similarly in golf. Since 1992 alone, the average drive of the top pro has extended from 260 yards to nearer 290-300.

After the gutty (*see page 48*), the next big breakthrough in golf occurred in 1898 when Coburn Haskell, a frustrated golfer, and Bertram Work, of the Goodrich Tire & Rubber Co., Akron, Ohio, patented what they thought was the world's first rubber core ball. It consisted of some 20 metres of rubber thread, machine-wound under tension around a solid vulcanised rubber core, and then covered by an outer layer of *gutta percha*.

In fact, as a court case in 1906 revealed, there had been earlier, unsuccessful Scottish versions. One of them, noted *The Scotsman*, 'had no click, and... golf without the click was, as one of the judges put it, not golf.'

But Haskell balls had that click, and as they also proved popular with less skilful golfers – that is, the majority – after several years of trials and debate, the rubber core ball prevailed to become the basis of all balls used throughout the 20th century (until a recent trend back to solids).

These four balls are a sample of the hundreds of variants made available from 1900-14, a time when architect-designed golf courses were opening up all over Britain. From top left they are, clockwise: a 1907 Challenger Star, by JP Cochrane of Edinburgh; a 1911 Olympic Special by FH Ayres of London; a 1910 Hex by Martins of Birmingham, and a Diamond Chick by the North British Rubber Co. of Edinburgh.

In 1936 *Golf Illustrated* stated, 'In 30 years the golf population of these islands has grown from some 100,000 to nearly 1,000,000 and golf has become an international sport. It is our view that the rubber cored ball has done for golf what the pneumatic tyre did for cycling and then motoring.'

Typical Diameter 4.3cm
Typical weight 42.5g

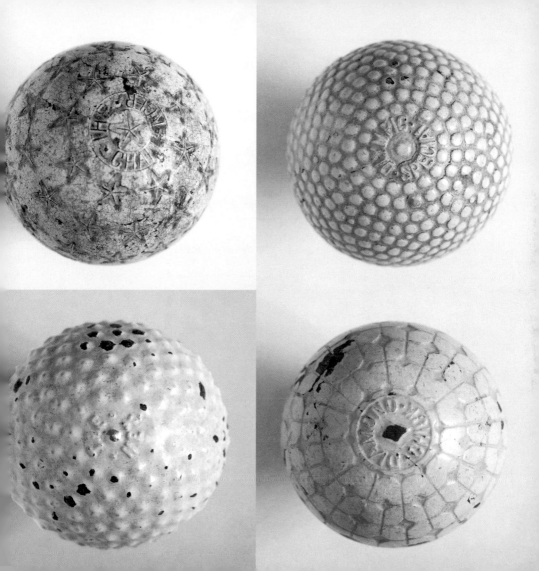

Shuttlecocks c.1911

Of all the sporting projectiles known to man, none appears more delicate than the shuttlecock. Yet wafted by an expert it can exceed speeds of over 150mph. On the other hand, it has been in development for rather longer than most balls.

First recorded in China around 500 BC and still played today in south east Asia – sometimes with feet rather than rackets – the shuttlecock has featured in European life since at least the 17th century. In Britain 'battledore and shuttlecock' was a genteel children's game in which players tried collectively to keep the shuttlecock off the ground for as long as possible, using long-handled bats with stretched vellum heads, called battledores.

The idea of striking the shuttlecock across a net, in competition, seems to have arisen first in France, around 1700, then again c.1860 at the Gloucestershire home of the Duke of Beaufort, Badminton House, where it was played indoors one rainy afternoon by officers on leave from the Indian army. As happened with snooker and polo, the rules were then honed in India and brought back to Britain as a fully developed sport in 1873.

Ever since, manufacturers have experimented with the shuttlecock; its cork base, its stitching, and the number and type of feathers. The current norm is 16 goose feathers (because of their high oil content, and therefore resilience). But as was discovered in the 1930s by studying shuttlecocks on film, to avoid uneven flight the feathers must be plucked all from a left wing or a right one.

These relatively hefty examples, by FH Ayres, date from between 1890 and 1911, when the Badminton Association first set standards for shuttlecocks. A typical modern shuttle weighs a much lighter 78-79 'grains' (in Troy weight).

In 1911 an Ayres shuttlecock cost 2s 11d and lasted, on average, for one game. Nowadays, a top quality shuttle costs £1, but with harder hitting, fitter players, does well to survive five or ten minutes. No wonder they stick to nylon ones down at the village hall.

Height 10cm
Weight 169 grains (11g)

Moorpool Estate, Harborne, Birmingham

Skittles 1913

In his role as chairman of Birmingham's Planning Committee, John Sutton Nettleford – a wealthy screw manufacturer – was a firm advocate of the Garden City movement, in which the provision of recreational facilities played a vital role. At the Moorpool Estate, for example, commissioned by Nettleford and designed by architects Martin & Martin, the 500 houses are ranged around a central core containing a tennis court, bowling

green and communal rooms. One of the latter features two 50 foot long skittle alleys, side by side; one flat (as is the norm), the other cambered (as is more common in Flanders but unknown elsewhere in Britain). Why this unique juxtaposition is a mystery. But then skittles has always been characterised by local idiocyncracies, and not even the formation of the Amateur Skittles Association in 1900 – a body later presided over by AP Herbert – led to any national standards.

The Moorpool 'woods' are of course lignum vitae, and are as old as the estate. The skittles, however, have to be replaced every decade or so. Note that there are ten. The tenth first appeared in Connecticut during the 1840s in order to circumvent laws that made nine-pin alleys illegal.

A rather longer tradition in skittles, maintained at Moorpool at least until the 1970s, was the payment of a few pennies to local boys to 'stack' the skittles after every bowler's 'end' (or turn). Hence the expression, earning pin money.

"Life isn't all beer and skittles; but beer and skittles, or something of the same sort, must form a good part of every Englishman's education."
Tom Brown's School Days, by Thomas Hughes, 1857

Largest diameter 21.6cm
Heaviest weight 6.35kg

Billie's Ball 1916

It was apparently Captain 'Billie' Nevill's idea. A ruse to divert his men from brooding over the task ahead – the capture of Montauban Ridge. For eight, ear-splitting, earth-shaking days, the Allied artillery had been pounding the enemy positions.

But now it was time. Nevill produced four footballs, daubing two with a message: 'The Great

European Cup-Tie Final, East Surreys v. Bavarians. Kick off at zero. No referee.'

The first platoon to score a goal in the enemy trenches, promised Nevill, would earn a reward.

At 7.27 the next morning, B Company climbed over the top into No Man's Land, Nevill and his second in command, Lt. RE Soames, at the fore, bayonets fixed, footballs at their feet.

In an instant the German machine guns tore through the East Surrey's ranks. But still, somehow, the balls were dribbled towards the distant trenches until the ridge was taken. Two of the balls were later found, close to the wire. As was Captain Nevill, shot through the head.

The Battle of the Somme was barely hours old, and yet already this was the bloodiest day ever in the history of the British Army. Some 57,000 were wounded, 19,000 lay dead. By mid November, casualties on both sides had exceeded 1.1 million.

Such slaughter defies comprehension. Yet this humble ball, returned to Blighty, invites us to try.

On through the hail of slaughter, where gallant comrades fall,
Where blood is poured like water, they drive the trickling ball.
The fear of death before them, is but an empty name;
True to the land that bore them, the Surreys played the game.
Touchstone, in the Daily Mail, July 1916

Diameter 21cm
Weight 410g

Lawn tennis balls 1922

Having originally relied on imports of rubber cores from Germany, Britain's tennis ball makers emerged from the Great War in patriotic mood. 'Buy Ayres and you buy British' was one slogan, while Slazenger, established in Manchester by the grandsons of immigrants from Silesia, stamped on their goods, 'Made Entirely in England.'

Joining them in this highly lucrative market were Gray's, Wisden, Spalding, Sykes and tyre makers Dunlop, from their huge Fort Dunlop works in Birmingham in 1918.

Slazenger had entered the business in 1885. But their biggest coup came in 1902 when they ousted Ayres as suppliers to Wimbledon. It later emerged that Slazenger were donating the balls for free, a revelation that forced the club secretary to resign. But he soon bounced back, as managing director of Slazenger, and the company has retained the Wimbledon contract ever since.

These unused balls from 1922 were among the last made with the Melton covers still stitched by hand. Thereafter, as shown at the Ayres factory in 1925 (*left*), covers were glued, thereby creating the familiar seam pattern that endures today.

Also dating from that era is the measurement of 'bound'. As established in 1924, when dropped from 100 inches onto a rigid surface a ball should bounce no less than 53 inches and no more than 58. Currently some 360 million tennis balls a year are produced to that standard, just one of many standards in international sport that can be truly said to have been 'Made Entirely in England'.

Diameter 6.2cm
Weight 58g

Stoolball 1923

Encountering a game of stoolball in the West Country in 1671, the antiquary John Aubrey noted, 'they smite a ball stuffed very hard with quills and covered with soale leather, with a staffe commonly made of withy, about three and half feet long.' The 'stobball ball,' he added, was about four inches in diameter and 'as hard as a stone'.

A mix of cricket and rounders, though predating both, stoolball is today one of Britain's longest surviving rural sports, almost as old as bowls.

First recorded in 1450, it features runs and overs, two teams of eleven players and two wickets (originally stools). Played by children, milkmaids and farmhands alike, it could be played on almost any field, level or not. Unlike cricket.

This stoolball, found recently in a biscuit tin in Plumpton, dates from c.1923, when Major WW Grantham set up the sport's first national body. The Major had started promoting stoolball as an aid to the rehabilitation of soldiers returning wounded from the Great War, his son included.

In homage to the game's rustic traditions Grantham always played in a smock, while newly emerging teams adopted lyrical names such as the Shrimps, the Bluebells and the Marigolds.

Like all stoolballs of the 1920s, this particular ball was originally manufactured for real tennis. Known as a 'Best Tennis Double Cover' and costing approximately 2s, it lasted twice as long as a normal ball, as its outer leather casing, once worn out, could be stripped off to reveal a second layer beneath. Hence the inner stitching, just visible to the left of the outer stitching.

Only later did companies such as Webber, John Jaques and Cliff make stoolballs specifically.

Nowadays the sport is played almost exclusively in Kent, Surrey, Sussex and Hampshire, and is classified by Sport England as 'a minor sport'. Not a view modern antiquaries would endorse. Stoolball is a quintessential part of our sporting heritage, with 5,000 players at over 200 clubs.

Long may they smite in the fields of England.

Diameter 60.5mm
Weight 70gms

Pushballs 1920s

Many a scientific breakthrough owes its origins to a happy accident. In 1839, Charles Goodyear's discovery of vulcanisation – without which mass production of hardwearing rubber balls would have been impossible – arose from a spillage in the workshop. In 1965 another American scientist, Norman Stingley, stumbled on the process that led to the Wham-O Superball; a ball so bouncy that no known game or garden fence could contain it.

A decade later came the Stress Ball, offering spongy relief to tense executives the world over.

Here were novelty balls in search of a role. In effect, chemical experiments with added spin.

Such a ball was the pushball – essentially a giant rubber bladder – as seen (*below left*) in Leyton, east London, in 1924. A team game sponsored by the *Daily Mail* was concocted to showcase its potential, at a time when new sports such as speedway, greyhound racing and ice hockey were all vying for public interest.

But if pushballs tended to deflate on land, on water they made a right splash. Often named after their sportswear sponsors, 'Bukta Balls' were to be seen bobbing about in Britain's lidos and open air swimming pools until at least the 1970s.

Of course they were never quite as easy to tame as made out by this detail from a poster for the South Bay open air pool in Scarborough (by an artist called Vandersyde). But that hardly stopped swimmers from trying.

Marbles 1932

Swapsies anyone? What are you after? A rainbow or an oily? A steely or a swirl? There's a mixed bag here: speckled German marbles from the 19th century, coloured French clay marbles from the 1920s, and cats eye and wire pull glass marbles from Japan and the Far East from the 1950s.

Marbles, of which precious few have actually been made from marble, have been with us for millennia, treasured by the Egyptians, Greeks, Romans and Aztecs alike. When St Paul spoke in Corinthians of the need to give up childish things, the Latin text uses *nuces*, alluding to the nuts played with by boys. In Twelfth Night, Sir Toby Belch jokes about Cherry Pit, a game played with cherry stones. Daniel Defoe wrote of alabaster globes, while in 1801 Joseph Strutt referred to the popular game of Taw, in which the aim was to knock your opponents' marbles out of a circle.

With the industrial age came mass production. In 1850 alone, 1600 cwt of aggies, or agate marbles, were imported from Germany via Hull.

Glass marbles from Germany followed after 1890, followed by American varieties after 1910. If nothing else they made excellent ballast.

Many of these imports would have found their way to the traditional heartland of British marbles, Sussex, where in April 1932 the first British Marbles Championships were staged outside the Greyhound Inn at Tinsley Green (filmed by Pathe News, no less). There it has remained ever since, competed for each Good Friday by teams such as the Tinsley Tigers and the Toucan Terribles.

Tales abound. Jim 'the Atomic Thumb' Longhurst, a Slaugham gardener and captain of the Handcross Bulldogs, could shatter a pint glass just by propelling his tolley – that is, his shooting marble – from a distance of four feet. Another hero was 'Pop' Maynard (*shown on page 96*), a folk singer and captain of the Copthorne Spitfires.

Apparently the secret is to have a strong thumb, and to rough up your tolley on a brick.

Now, who's in for Allies?

On yon gray stone that fronts the chancel-door,
Worn smooth by busy feet, now seen no more,
Each eve we shot the marble through the ring
When the heart danced, and life was in its spring.
Pleasures of Memory, by Samuel Rogers, 1792

Catford, London

Snowballs 1947

For over seven weeks in 1947, from January to March, snow fell every day in at least one part of the British Isles. Just what a war weary nation needed in the midst of acute food and coal shortages, though affording to these London schoolboys, at least, optimum conditions for the perfect snowball. According to meteorologists, these occur at between 0-1°C, at which point snowflakes are larger, settle for longer, yet melt just enough to meld the snow into a satisfyingly compact and aerodynamic missile.

Similar conditions greeted members of the South London Swimming Club during their annual Christmas swim at Tooting Bec Lido (*left*), during the next Big Freeze of 1962-63. Over 400 football matches were called off that winter. The 3rd Round of the FA Cup took 66 days to complete.

But are our snowballing days over? In the early 19th century crowds of 10,000 would gather along frozen canals in the Fens to watch speed skating races between farm labourers. In the 1890s Londoners could skate outdoors for 15 days a year on average. Whereas now we ski down artificial slopes and place increasingly forlorn bets on the likelihood of a white Christmas.

The forecast then? Unsettled. General snowfall is definitely down. But isolated bouts of heavy snow are apparently on the up, though much less likely to settle as overall temperatures rise.

In summary: make snowballs before the sun shines. And as for packing them with ice and aiming for the neck – well, as if you would.

Snowy, Flowy, Blowy,
Showery, Flowery, Bowery,
Hoppy, Croppy, Droppy,
Breezy, Sneezy, Freezy
The 12 months of the year, George Ellis , 1753-1815

Challenge Cup Final Replay ball 1954

No-one is sure if the mouldering ball reportedly found at the Thrum Hall ground in Halifax in 1988 – ten years before its demolition – is *the* ball. But it certainly predates 1960, when rugby league switched from a four panel to a six panel ball, and if Halifax were to keep any ball from their past, the one from the Challenge Cup Final Replay, staged at Odsal Stadium, Bradford, on 5 May 1954, would have been a prime contender.

For that was a night enshrined in the annals of rugby league; a night on which, against all expectations and despite heavy rain – let alone the rival appeal of Laurel and Hardy at the nearby Alhambra – an unprecedented 102,569 fans turned up to see Warrington beat Halifax 8-4. And that was just the official count. In truth some 120,000, at least, squeezed onto Odsal's vast, cinder slopes, as wave after wave of humanity overwhelmed the ground's flimsy outer fences.

But why the frenzy on that particular night? Until then Odsal's record stood at 70,000. In the Final itself, played at Wembley four days earlier, the gate had been just under 82,000. Not even a full house, and not much of a game either.

Yet such were the crowds for the replay that the ball's supplier, Arthur Clues, only just made it from his Leeds shop in time, thanks to a police escort, while thousands of fans ended up trapped on gridlocked roads – no motorways then – desperate to find any vehicle with a radio. Those who arrived late, meanwhile, saw precious little of the action. Remarkably, despite the potentially disastrous collapse of several barriers, only two people were hospitalised and there were no reports of any disorder on the night.

Not that the London press seemed interested. Instead, the following day all eyes turned to Iffley Road, Oxford, where some university chaps were attempting to run a four minute mile. Within hours the whole world had learnt of Roger Bannister's feat. Odsal's world record, by contrast, caused barely a stir south of the Pennines.

Length c.28cm
Diameter at centre c.59cm
Weight c.420g

Health and Efficiency magazine

Beachball 1955/1962

Call it what you will. A sexist cliché. A female fig-leaf. A ball of oppression, or a ball of liberation.

But the beachball was more than just a cheap rubber or plastic plaything; more than a convenient prop for photographers. Sport and naturism have always been closely allied. Enid Blyton is said to have enjoyed a round of tennis in the nude, while today one can join naturist clubs for cycling, rambling, running, even ski-ing and sky-diving, Most shockingly of all, there is a nudists' swimming club in Edinburgh which, in 2002, apparently threatened to pose for a fundraising calender, fully clothed.

Since it espoused the cause during the 1930s, the journal *Health and Efficiency* (incorporating *Health & Vim* magazine) – founded in 1900 and the only monthly commercial naturist magazine in the world today – has provided a sober, if often airbrushed window onto the world of British naturism (as few males over the age of 50 will need reminding).

As for the magazine's penchant for inflatable balls, all is revealed in the July 1955 issue.

Why, asks Hugh, a visitor to one club, do members play obscure games seldom seen elsewhere, rather than, say, tennis?

Replies Jim, a committee member, 'It's largely a matter of resources. Space and £ s d.'

A tennis court, he explains, takes up an awful lot of room, something few British naturist clubs have in abundance. It requires upkeep too, and his committee have quite enough on their plates as it is. Also, only four can play at any one time.

Besides which, 'tennis breeds its own kind of snobbery: the proficient player despises the rabbit and is impatient during every minute that beginners occupy the court.'

'We ought never to let such a tendency creep in,' insists Jim. At his club they prefer games that everyone can play, on a more friendly and casual basis, regardless of skill.

Like beachball and volleyball for instance.

HEALTH
AND
EFFICIENCY
JULY :: 1955
ONE SHILLING

KIRBY

THE WORLD'S LEADING NATURIST JOURNAL Est. 1900

HEALTH
and
EFFICIENCY
JANUARY 2'6

PHYSICAL FITNESS
MENTAL FITNESS
HEALTH & BEAUTY

Now **100** Pages
FUN IN THE SUN
WONDERFUL PICTURES

Tenpin bowling 1960

Picked out by an *Evening Standard* photographer in December 1960 and clutching a standard, black rubber ball of the day – manufactured by AMF, the American Machine and Foundry Co. of New York – 18 year old shorthand typist, June Campbell, was one youngster among many swept up by Britain's newest sporting craze.

Tenpin was skittles for the space age; the alley electrified, courtesy of the automated pinspotter, invented by Fred Schmidt in his garage in Pear River NY in 1936.

Britain's first pinspotters were installed at US air bases during the mid 1950s. AMF then opened their first public alley at an ABC cinema in Stamford Hill in January 1960. Hollywood heart-throb Douglas Fairbanks Junior, who had earned 'pin money' as a boy and who was now on the AMF board, hosted the gala opening. Everest climber Sir John Hunt bowled the inaugural ball – a gilded one, naturally – straight into the gutter, before scoring a strike on his second ball.

Following him were cricket's Bedser twins and the actors Stanley Baker and Carole Lesley.

Within months Top Rank were gutting cinemas all over London to meet demand. Stamford Hill became a regular haunt for the Spurs' Double winning team every Monday night. A club formed there called the Chipmunks. Luton's club was the Sputniks. By 1965 over 40,000 bowlers had signed up nationwide.

Around that time specks of colour started appearing on the balls. AMF and their rivals, Brunswick, then introduced Ebonite. In the 1980s brightly coloured Urethane balls took over. By then, however, Top Rank had abandoned tenpin for bingo. Yet despite this, there are now over 200 alleys in Britain, the highest number ever.

With their refined composition and accurately weighted bias, today's balls skim across the hard lacquered lanes with ever greater velocity and turn. But not at Stamford Hill. A supermarket now occupies that once star-studded corner.

Diameter 21.6cm
Weight 4.5-7.3kgs

Football Association Challenge Cup Committee

FA Cup Draw 1964

In the early days, numbered scraps of paper were pulled out of a top hat behind closed doors, whilst invited members of the press, and seemingly every other staff member at the Football Association, waited eagerly in the corridor to hear the outcome.

Then in 1935 the BBC decided to broadcast the 3rd Round draw, the stage of the tournament at which the 'big boys' join the 'minnows'.

FA Secretary Stanley Rous was requested 'to produce a distinctive sound' for listeners. Polished hardwood balls being shaken in a velvet bag made just such a sound. Subtle, but tantalising.

The BBC hedged its bets. 'This broadcast is an experiment,' it emphasised.

But the experiment ran for 50 years, bringing to a halt factories and offices at shortly after midday on the second or third Monday of every December. Under desks and in toilet cubicles schoolboys across the nation huddled around transistor radios.

For the 4th Round draw in January 1964 (*left*) the plum tie was an East End derby, Leyton Orient v. West Ham, the eventual winners.

More recently nylon balls in a glass bowl have taken over, and the draw is televised at weekends. But the old balls, 128 in total, and their bag, dating from the 1970s, are still in regular use for the seven other FA competitions drawn in private.

And they still make that delicious clacking sound that once set a million hearts racing.

Diameter 3cm
Weight 10g

The Braemar stone 1965

On a dour September day, watched by 20,000 hardy souls – the Queen and most of her close family included – local farmer Robert Shaw steps up to the trig (the marker) and prepares for 'putting the stone'. As the Braemar Gathering rules require, he wears a kilt of the family clan and, unlike at other Highland Games, throws from a standing position, with no run-up or turns.

In his grip is a smooth lump, not quite oval, not quite round. Picked from the bed of a nearby river – no-one is quite sure when (50 years ago, maybe more) – this is the Braemar 28 pounder. Every Highland Games has one similar, hewn over thousands of years by the rushing waters.

Shaw heaves, but it is not enough. A rival has managed a distance of 38 feet and 2.5 inches, a new record for this most ancient of events.

They call this part of the Braemar Gathering 'the Heavies', and with good reason. In addition to putting the stone there is throwing the weight, throwing the hammer and, best known of all, tossing the caber. In another Heavy event contestants hurl a 56lb weight over a raised bar; a task once likened to throwing a seven year old boy over a double decker bus... with one hand.

Elsewhere in the biting wind there are contests for Highland dancing and piping, a tug-of-war and the annual foot race, up the punishing slopes of Murrone, overlooking the village of Braemar.

It is a programme little changed since first staged in 1832, although the tradition of gatherings is said to go back to the 8th century. Queen Victoria loved to attend so much that its timing was fixed to suit her and her entourage, up in Scotland since the start of the grouse shooting season on the Glorious 12th (of August).

As it happens, the current record for putting the Braemar stone – 40 feet and 10 inches, in 1981 – is held by the Sassenach strongman, Geoff Capes. Once again, Caledonia has had to bow to Albion's might. But this a long game. For the old stone of Braemar will surely outlive us all.

Diameter 20.3cm
Weight 12.7kg

World Cup football 1966

'I can't believe how passionate you can be about a little old football,' Helmut Haller told the *Daily Mirror* as he handed over the famed 1966 World Cup ball to England's hat-trick hero Geoff Hurst at a secret location in Essex. Haller had been storing the ball in his Augsburg cellar, apparently oblivious to the fact that for 30 years Geoff, and, seemingly the entire English nation, had been asking, 'Can we have our ball back mister?'

It had taken *Mirror* reporters two days of hard bargaining in the midst of a media frenzy, followed by car chases and fisticuffs involving rival sleuths from *The Sun*. But now, after Haller had accepted a reported £70,000 in charity donations from the *Mirror*, Eurostar and Virgin combined, the ball was back just in time for the Euro '96 Championships in England, a tournament whose theme tune was aptly titled 'Football's Coming Home'.

But why did the former German midfielder have the ball in the first place?

Haller, who had netted the opening goal in the 1966 Final, insisted that it was a German tradition for the first goalscorer to claim the match ball. But in England a more celebrated tradition assigns that right to any player scoring a hat-trick.

Even so, amid the wild celebrations that ensued on that sun-kissed afternoon in July 1966, no-one in the England camp had stopped Haller from clutching the ball as he received his loser's medal from the Queen, in full view of the watching millions. Nor had there been any complaints when he asked several England players to sign it at the post-match banquet that same evening.

Those signatures have long since faded, but the iconic ball – a 24 panel model handmade by a Slazenger employee, Malcolm Wainwright – retains far more than its amber glow. For this is English football's Holy Grail, a symbol of victory, or, as one dewy-eyed observer noted after the ball's return, the embodiment of our Faustian desire not to let a 'beautiful moment' fade away.

Diameter 22.2cm
Weight 425g

Fives balls 1996

To understand fives – a direct descendant of the medieval *jeu de paume* – in which gloved hands, rather than rackets, strike the ball against a wall, we have to play the numbers game.

At the last count, some 30 versions of this kind of handball have been identified in 50 countries. In Britain there are three types, each codified by public schools in the 19th century; Eton Fives, in which two pairs compete in a three-sided court (complete with mock buttress to echo the school's chapel walls), and Rugby Fives and Winchester Fives, which both feature four sided courts.

However an earlier form of fives, played in the West Country, used only one wall, and usually a church wall at that. Several in Somerset and Dorset still bear the scars. (As noted earlier, the Scots called their version of handball caich.)

There are four theories as to how fives got its name, the most likely being that all five digits are called into action. But for the history of fives balls we need look no further than the Graham Turnbull trophy, created in 1996. The three on the left are early 20th century, their cork cores wrapped with felt, tied with twine and covered in hand-sewn kid leather. Their makers are thought to be Malings of London (*far left*) and either Gradidge or Slazenger.

Second from the right is a 1970s Rugby Fives ball made by Jabez Cliff of Walsall, its core soaked in liquid rubber and its seams glued.

The fifth example (*far right*) is a modern Eton Fives ball, made from a rubber and cork composite introduced after much experimentation in the 1960s. More durable and rounder than all its predecessors, its greater zip has helped fives enjoy a revival. J Price of Bath made the one shown here, while Cliff, and G6 of Devon, continue to manufacture balls for Rugby Fives.

That there should still be three British ball makers supplying such a relatively minor sport is in itself noteworthy. But with around 330 courts between the three fives codes, and rising, the numbers soon add up.

Diameter 4.45cm
Weight 40g

THE GRAHAM TURNBULL TROPHY

Rugby World Cup Final ball 2003

Just like Geoff Hurst in '66, England hero Jonny Wilkinson somehow contrived to leave the scene of his World Cup winning triumph in Sydney in November 2003 without the match ball. Or rather, without any one of the five balls used during that most auspicious of games (won by England in the final seconds, courtesy of a Wilkinson drop goal).

Instead, one of the five was reportedly spirited away by a fan – rumour has it from Wigan – when Jason Robinson punched the ball into the crowd in delight after scoring a 38th minute try. The other four, each signed by the referee as proof of authenticity, were handed over to a Sydney firm, Legends Genuine Memorabilia, who had bought the rights to the balls beforehand and offered them as prizes in a ballot costing around £400 a pop.

But when one of the winners put his ball up for sale on e-Bay days later – amid reports that it could fetch up to £500,000 – the scent was laid...

In 1996 it fell to the *Daily Mirror* to bring home Geoff Hurst's hat-trick ball from Germany. In December 2003 it was the turn of *The Sun*.

But which of the four was the match winner?

Off to Sydney a crack team of Wapping's finest pleading Poms thus jetted, cheque books in hand. Three of the ball winners were soon persuaded. A fourth, self-confessed 'memorabilia nut' played harder to get, finally settling for two other signed balls in return. Then it was back to Blighty, with all four Gilberts strapped into the very same seat Wilkinson had occupied weeks earlier on an aptly named British Airways Jumbo, Sweet Chariot.

'Delighted Jonny, 24,' was presented with one of the balls by the jubilant *Sun*. Captain Martin Johnson received another, as did a *Sun* competition winner, weeks later. The fourth – shown here – is on display in the Museum of Rugby at Twickenham.

But which was the actual one Jonny kicked for victory? No one, it seems, will ever know for sure.

Length 29cm
Diameter at centre 19.1cm
Weight 435g

Kirkwall Ba' Committee, Orkney

Kirkwall ba' 2003

The one thing onlookers, and indeed most of the participants see very little of during the Kirkwall Ba' game is the ba' itself.

Having been ceremonially tossed into the waiting throng of Uppies and Doonies – the two rival teams – at 1pm by the Market Cross, the ba' might resurface only at the final moment of victory, such as witnessed here, at just after 5pm on Christmas Day, 2003, a month after England's triumph in the Rugby World Cup.

The two games are of course close cousins. Yet whereas Jonny Wilkinson, for all his fame and acclaim, failed to hang onto his match-winning ball, as is Orcadian tradition, 37 year old Raymie Stanger (in the red shirt) got to keep his forever.

An Uppie by birth and a joiner by trade, Stanger has no prouder possession. For in common with the balls used in Britain's other surviving mass football games (such as at Ashbourne, Atherstone and Workington), the Kirkwall ba' is as beautifully crafted as it is imbued in centuries of tradition.

It is also necessarily robust, kicking and running with the ba' having been replaced by handling and scrimmaging during the 1830s.

Each ba' takes four days to make, and as they are never re-used, every year Kirkwall's ba' makers must provide four new ones, for both the boys' and mens' games, each played on Christmas and New Year's Day. (Until 1855 every couple getting married in Kirkwall had to contribute to the ba' making fund. Nowadays collections suffice.)

Each ba' consists of an eight panel leather casing, stitched together using extra-strong flax, and then stuffed tightly with cork dust, which used to be scraped from the grape barrels of local fruiterers but is now imported from Portugal.

The leather is then stained in brown and black decorative patterns (as seen on back cover).

Until recently winners frequently hung their ba' in their front window, for passers-by to admire. But Raymie keeps his in a display cabinet in the sitting room, where he gives it a regular polish.

Diameter 22.6cm
Weight 1.36kg

Real tennis ball 2005

Though it may seem paradoxical to conclude our trawl through the old balls of Britain with one made in 2005, we are concerned here not with the ball as such, but with its place in history.

On page 18 we learnt how, during the 16th century, the art of making tennis balls had to adapt to suit the game's transition from a form of handball to a racket sport. In essence, there have been few changes since. True, the materials have been updated, for example the use of Optic Yellow Melton covers for extra visibility. Otherwise, the French authority, François de Garsault – author of a definitive guide to ballmaking in 1767 – would recognise instantly the methods, and even the tools used in any one of the 23 real tennis clubs in Britain today. Not only that, he would also note, perhaps with some sympathy, that, as in his era, the person responsible for making the balls (as well as repairing rackets, coaching beginners and managing the court), is the club professional.

In no other sport are senior players so put upon.

At Hampton Court, where the tennis court dates from 1626, the professional, Chris Ronaldson, uses cork fragments for the core of his balls, though others use rags. (Army uniforms were once apparently popular too). First he wraps the cork in bits of used Melton, forming a tight ball, tied with mattress twine (*top left*). He then pounds this core with a hammer, wraps it a second time in cotton webbing, before tying the whole in more twine, and pounding it again in a metal ball-cup to create the required size (*top right*). Two strips of new Melton are then tacked on (*bottom left*) and their seams hand-sewn for the final ball (*bottom right*).

Each ball takes 40 minutes to make from scratch, or 20 if a used core is recycled. To meet demand, Ronaldson and his two assistants need to make 6-8 balls a day. It is arduous work.

Of course machine-made alternatives have been tried. But while in other arenas we hear the cry go up, 'New balls please,' in real tennis, it would seem, the oldest balls in sport still do just fine.

Diameter 62-65mm
Weight 71-78g

Links

General history

Arlott J (ed) *The Oxford Companion to Sports and Games* Oxford University Press (1976)
Baker Dr C *Natural Rubber – History and Developments* Materials World, Vol 5, No 1 (January 1997)
Burnett J *Riot, Revelry and Rout: Sport in Lowland Scotland Before 1860* Tuckwell Press (2000)
Cox R, Jarvie G & Vamplew W (eds) *Encyclopedia of British Sport* ABC-CLIO (2000)
Dean C *Slazenger - the Founders of the Company* (booklet 2003)
Glasson M *Walsall Leather Industry – The World's Saddlers* Tempus (2003)
Jarvie G & Burnett J (eds) *Sport, Scotland and the Scots* Tuckwell Press 2000
Kaufman M *The First Century of Plastics* Plastics and Rubber Society Institute (1963)
Moore K *Museums and Popular Culture* Leicester University Press (1997)
Strutt J *The Sports and Pastimes of the People of England* Firecrest Publishing (1801, reprinted 1969)

Billiards

Clare N *Billiards and Snooker Bygones* Shire Publications (1996)
Shamos M *The Complete Book of Billiards – A Fully Illustrated Reference Guide to the World of Billiards, Pool, Snooker and other Cue Sports* Gramercy Books (1993)

Bowls and skittles

Armstrong P & Ayers B *Excavations in High Street and Blackfriargate* East Riding Archaeologist Vol 8 (1987)
Clare P *History of Bowls and other articles* World Bowls (1997-98) & Today's Bowler (2003)
Morris CA *Craft, Industry and Everyday Life: Wood and Woodworking in Anglo-Scandinavian and Medieval York* The Archaeology of York Vol 17, York Archaeological Trust (2000)
Tunnicliffe T *London Skittles – A Lost Recreation* (research paper 1987)

Cricket

Barty-King H *Quilt Winders and Pod Shavers – The History of Cricket Bat and Ball Manufacturers* Macdonald and Jane's (1979)
Rice T *Treasures of Lord's* Willow Books (1989)

Croquet
All England Croquet Club *Croquet, Its Implements and Laws* Horace Cox (1869)
Prichard DMC *The History of Croquet* Cassell (1981)

Football
Allen P *An Amber Glow – The Story of England's World Cup-Winning Football* Mainstream (2000)
Mayes H *World Cup Report* Football Association & William Heinemann (1966)

Golf
McGimpsey K *The Story of the Golf Ball* Philip Wilson (2003)

Kirkwall Ba'
Robertson JDM *The Kirkwall Ba' – Between the Water and the Wall* Dunedin Academic Press (2005)

Marbles and Carpet Bowls
Baumann P *Collecting Antique Marbles. Identification and Price Guide* KP Books (2004)

Rugby League
Gate R *"There Were A Lot More Than That"- Odsal 1954* (1994)

Rugby Union
Gilbert J *Rugby Football – the Gilbert Story* James Gilbert (1957)
Ray D *From Webb Ellis to World Cup* Rugby School (1991)

Stoolball
National Stoolball Association *Stoolball – The Game, Rules, History* (booklet 1993)

Subbuteo
Tatarsky D *Flick to Kick - an illustrated history of Subbuteo* Orion (2004)

Tennis
Lord Aberdare *The JT Faber Book of Tennis & Rackets* Quiller Press (2001)
Gillmeister H *Tennis – A Cultural History* Leicester University Press (1997)
Morgan R *Tennis: The Development of the European Ball Game* Ronaldson Publications (1995)
Simpson B & Barty-King H *Friends at Court - Wimbledon & Slazenger since 1902* Quiller Press (2002)

Websites – sports

www.badmintonengland.co.uk
www.bagame.com
www.bowlsengland.com
www.braemargathering.org
www.btba.org.uk
www.croquet.org.uk
www.croquetworld.co.uk
www.etonfives.co.uk
www.harrowschool.org.uk
www.londonskittles.co.uk
www.marblemuseum.org/tinsley
www.randa.org
www.realtennis.gbrit.com
www.realtennisonline.com
www.rfa.org.uk
www.rfl.uk.com
www.rlhalloffame.org.uk
www.rugbyschool.net
www.stoolball.co.uk
www.thefa.com

Websites – museums and collections

www.britishgolfmuseum.co.uk
www.golfballmuseum.co.uk
www.hullcc.gov.uk/museums/hulleast
www.ittf.com/museum
www.lords.org/history/mcc-museum
www.museumoflondon.org.uk
www.nationalfootballmuseum.com
www.nms.ac.uk/scotland/home
www.peter-upton.co.uk/sub1.htm
www.queensroyalsurreys.org.uk
www.rfu.com/microsites/museum
www.scarboroughmuseums.org.uk
www.smithartgallery.demon.co.uk
www.st-andrews.ac.uk/services/muscoll/home.htm
www.vam.ac.uk/vastatic/nmc
www.walsall.gov.uk/leathermuseum
www.webb-ellis.co.uk
www.wimbledon.org/en_GB/about/museum
www.yorkcastlemuseum.org.uk

Websites – manufacturers and retailers

www.dunlopsports.com
www.g6sports.ndirect.co.uk
www.glovesandballs.com
www.grays-int.co.uk
www.jaques.co.uk
www.jpricebath.co.uk
www.mastersgames.com
www.thomas-taylor.co.uk
www.thurston-games.co.uk
www.tradgames.org.uk

A plastic coated cricket ball from the late 1940s, as supplied to schools and clubs all over Britain and the colonies by the Walsall manufacturers, Jabez Cliff and Co.

Credits

Photographs

Ken Amer: back cover, left, 87; David Brearley: 39; British Golf Museum: 49, 53; Jabez Cliff & Co Ltd: 11; Craig Eccleston: back cover, right, 93; English Heritage, Nigel Corrie: 8, 27, 37, 61, 67, 77, 85; English Heritage, James Davies: 12, 44, 45, 56, 57; Getty Images: inside front cover, 2, 60, 64, 69, 75, 76, 79, 96; Grays International Ltd: 7; H&E Naturist: 73; Hull & East Riding Museum, Hull Museums & Art Gallery: 15; The Illustrated London News: 58; Simon Inglis: inside back cover, 4, 13, 24, 25, 35, 51, 55, 63, 89; © ITTF Museum 2005: back cover, centre,1, 47; Paul Lapsley, 31; Peter Learoyd: 71; Manchester United FC Museum: cover; Andrew Mardell: 83; Queen's Royal Surrey Regiment Museum: 59; Roger Matile: 33; © Museum of London: 19; National Football Museum: 41, 43, 81; © The Royal and Ancient Golf Club of St Andrews: 29; Scarborough Museums & Gallery: 65; © Smith Art Gallery & Museum: 21; South London Swimming Club: 68; Thomas Taylor (Bowls) Ltd: 9; © The Trustees of the National Museums of Scotland: 17; © University of St Andrews: 23; V&A Images/Museum of Childhood: 67; Webb Ellis Rugby Football Museum: 10

Acknowledgements

The author and English Heritage wish to thank the following individuals for their invaluable assistance: Tony Alcock, English Bowling Association; Sara Backhouse, H & E Naturist; Paul Baumann and Roger Matile, carpet bowls; David Best, Brian Rich and Chris Ronaldson, real tennis; Hannah Betts, Lancing College; Claire Bradley, Webb Ellis Museum, Rugby; Jill Brill, National Badminton Museum; David Buchanan, Scarborough Museum and Art Gallery; Chris Buck, Airport Bowl; John Burnett and George Dalgliesh, National Museum of Scotland; Mark Bushell, Peter Holme and Malcolm MacCallum, National

Football Museum; Professor Ian Carradice and David Hopes, St Andrew's University; Ian Chatfield, David Swan and Col Les Wilson, Queen's Royal Surrey Regiment Museum; Peter Clare, EA Clare & Son Group Ltd; Steve Clark, Football Association; John Collier, Old Trafford Bowling Club; Tony Collins, Rugby League; David Drazin and Christopher Moore, croquet; Mike Fenn and Howard Wiseman, Eton Fives Association; Martin Foreman, Hull & East Riding Museum; Hazel Forsyth, Museum of London; Mike Glasson, Walsall Leather Museum; Matthew Glaze, Wimbledon Tennis Museum; Richard Gray, Grays International Ltd; Lizzie Hazlehurst, British Golf Museum: Chuck Hoey, International Table Tennis Federation Museum; Catherine Howell, Museum of Childhood; Ken Howells, hockey; Dilip Jajodia, Morrant Group Ltd; Steve Beauchampe, Peter Jordan and Mick O'Malley, Morpool Estate; Elspeth King, Smith Art Gallery and Museum; Cliff Kirby-Tibbits, Jabez Cliff & Co Ltd; Jenny Mann, City of Lincoln Archaeology Unit; Peter Maxton, Reinforced Shuttlecocks Ltd; Richard McBrearty, Scottish Football Museum; Sam McCarthy-Fox, British Marbles Board of Control; William Meston, Braemar Royal Highland Society; Carole Morris; Michelle Petyt, York Castle Museum; Kay and John Price, National Stoolball Association; Eve Skorski and Paul MacCallum, Barnes Bowling Club; Jed Smith and Laura Stedman, Museum of Rugby, Twickenham; Marie Sutherland, S & JD Roberston Group, Kirkwall; Peter Upton, subbuteo; Ian Urquhart, Thomas Taylor Bowls Ltd; Dale Vargas, Harrow School; Rosemary Weinstein; Dr Richard Wild, Weathernet; Glenys Williams, MCC Museum

Next page **Eighty year old Pop Maynard of the Copthorne Spitfires and his 51 year old son Arthur compete in the British Marbles Championships outside the Greyhound Inn, Tinsley Green, West Sussex, in April 1952. The Championships have been held at the pub every Good Friday since 1932 and are based on the traditional marbles game of Ring Taw.**